The Big Book of Self-Defence Made Easy for Kids

Priyanka Verma

AF651718

DIAMOND BOOKS

www.diamondbooks.in

Publisher : **Diamond Pocket Books (P) Ltd.**
X-30, Okhla Industrial Area, Phase-II
New Delhi-110020
Phone : 011-40712200
E-mail : wecare@diamondbooks.in
Website : www.diamondbooks.in
Edition : 2025
Printed By : Repro (India)

Preface

Dear Readers,

Welcome to The Big Book of Self-Defence Made Easy for Kids! This book is designed especially for young learners like you—curious, brave, and ready to take on the world with confidence.Self-defence doesn't mean fighting. It means knowing how to stay safe, trust your instincts, use your voice, protect your space, and stay alert. In today's world, where children are often independent in school, playgrounds, buses, and online spaces, learning self-defence is just as important as learning math or science.This book follows India's National Education Policy (NEP) 2020 and is packed with activities, games, stories, and real-life lessons that will help you become smarter, stronger, and safer.
So, get ready to explore, learn, and grow—because your safety is your superpower!

With care,

- Priyanka Verma

Foreword

“Children are the heart of our nation. Equipping them with safety skills is as essential as literacy. This book makes self-defence accessible, positive, and practical for children. It aligns beautifully with the spirit of NEP 2020 by promoting life skills, confidence, and emotional resilience. I recommend every parent, school, and teacher to include this in their learning journey.”

Contents

Chapter 1

What Is Self-Defence?

Have you ever felt a little nervous walking alone down a hallway at school? Or maybe someone at the park started following you or teasing you? Did you freeze, run, or tell someone? These are real-life situations where knowing how to protect yourself becomes very important.

Let's meet Aarav and Meher. Aarav was walking home from the bus stop when he noticed a group of older boys staring and whispering. They didn't do anything, but Aarav felt uneasy. Meher was at a birthday party, and someone she didn't know tried to hold her hand and pull her to dance. She didn't want to, but she didn't know how to say no.

What could Aarav and Meher have done?

That's what self-defence is all about.

Explore

What Does Self-Defence Really Mean?

Self-defence means keeping yourself safe from harm or danger. It's not just about fighting or kicking someone. In fact, it mostly involves using your mind, voice, and body in smart ways so that you don't get into dangerous situations at all.

Here's a simple definition:
"Self-defence is using everything you know—your awareness, actions, and voice—to protect yourself from anything or anyone that tries to hurt you."

Self-defence can include:
• Saying "NO" in a strong voice
• Staying away from danger
• Telling a trusted adult
• Running to safety
• Blocking or stopping someone's hand
• Yelling to get attention

Why Should Kids Learn Self-Defence?
Children like you go to school, play outside, travel in buses, go to coaching or activity classes, and even attend online classes. In all these spaces, you meet many people. Most are kind and friendly, but some might try to harm, bully, or scare you.

Learning self-defence:
• Builds your confidence
• Helps you make quick and safe decisions
• Teaches you how to trust your instincts
• Keeps your mind and body strong
• Helps you stay calm in tough situations
Self-Defence ≠ Fighting

Many people think self-defence means fighting. But that's wrong. Self-defence is not about hurting others—it's about protecting yourself and learning how to stay out of harm's way. Fighting is usually the last thing anyone should do.

Let's look at a few everyday examples:

Situation	Smart Self-Defence Response
Someone blocks your way in school	Step aside, say "Excuse me", walk confidently
A stranger asks you to go somewhere	Say "No", walk away quickly, tell a trusted adult
Someone tries to grab your bag	Hold tight, yell "Help!", run to a crowd
You feel uncomfortable near someone	Move away, talk to your parents or teacher

Try It

Here are some self-defence awareness activities you can try with your friends, parents, or teachers.

Role Play: Yes or No?
Ask someone to act out different situations. You respond with a "Yes" or "No" and explain why.

For example:
- Giving a friend a high five (Yes)
- A stranger asking you to come to their car (No)
- A teacher asking you to stay back alone after class (No – unless a parent knows)

Safety Walk
Take a walk around your home, school, or neighbourhood.

Identify:
- Safe places (guard's cabin, a friend's house, school gate)
- Unsafe spots (dark alley, empty building, closed shops)
- People you can trust (teacher, policeman, bus driver)

Strong Voice Practice

Practice saying these phrases in a firm and loud voice:

- "Stop! I don't like that."
- "Leave me alone."
- "I'm calling my parents."
- "Help! I need help!"

Think & Reflect

Let's ask ourselves some deep questions:

- What does safety mean to you?
- Who are the people you trust and why?
- Do you think being alert can stop danger before it starts?
- If your friend is being bullied, how can you use self-defence to help them?

Let's Revise

Here are the Top 5 Things to Remember:

1. Self-defence is for everyone – boys, girls, young or old.
2. It starts in the mind – awareness is your first superpower.
3. Use your voice, eyes, and feet before you ever need your hands.
4. Telling someone is not tattling—it's protecting.
5. Avoiding danger is smarter than facing it head-on.

Check Yourself

Test your learning with this short quiz.

Multiple Choice (Tick the Correct Answer):

1. Self-defence means:
    - Hitting someone back
    - Keeping yourself safe ✔
    - Ignoring the situation

2. What should you do if you feel unsafe?
    - Stay silent
    - Tell a trusted adult ✔
    - Keep it to yourself

3. Which of the following is a good way to defend yourself?
    - Pretend to laugh it off
    - Walk away and tell someone ✔
    - Hit the person hard

True or False:
4. Self-defence always means punching. **False**
5. Walking away from a bully is weak. **False**
6. Using your voice is part of self-defence. **True**
7. You should never talk about unsafe touches. **False**

Creative Corner:
Draw a comic strip showing a kid using self-defence skills to stay safe in three panels.

Beyond the Book

Here are some real-world tasks and challenges for you!

Project: My Safety Circle

Make a chart or poster with the names and pictures of people you can go to when you feel unsafe:
- Parents
- Teachers
- Neighbours
- School guard
- Elder siblings

Put this chart on your bedroom wall or in your school folder.

Movie Time
Watch a child-friendly animated video on personal safety.

Every morning, look in the mirror and say:
"I am smart. I am strong. I will stay safe."

Real-Life Inspirations

Real Story:
Zoya, a 9-year-old in Mumbai, was waiting outside her dance class when a man tried to grab her hand. She screamed loudly, pushed him, and ran into the building. The man ran away.

Zoya said, "I remembered what I learned about yelling and running. I'm glad I didn't freeze."
Lesson: Self-defence is not about being the biggest. It's about being the bravest and smartest in the room.

Words to Learn (Glossary)

- Awareness: Being alert and noticing what's around you
- Trusted Adult: Someone you can go to when you're scared
- Danger: Something that can hurt you or make you feel unsafe
- Instinct: The feeling inside you that says something isn't right
- Self-Defence: Protecting yourself using your mind, body, and voice

Chapter 2

My Body Is My Own

Aanya was at a family wedding. Her parents were busy, and a distant uncle tried to hug and kiss her even though she didn't feel comfortable. Aanya wriggled away and ran to her older sister. Later, when she told her mother, her mother said, "You did the right thing. Your body is your own. You have the right to say no."

The very next day at school, Aanya's class teacher began a new lesson on safety. It was called: "My Body is My Own."

Let's learn what Aanya did right—and how you can, too.

Explore

What Does "My Body Is My Own" Mean?

It means that you are the boss of your body.

No one—absolutely no one—has the right to touch your body, tickle you, or hug you if you don't want them to.

You are in charge of your body, and you have the right to say:

"I don't like that."

"Please stop."
"That makes me uncomfortable."
"No, thank you."

This also means:

- You decide who can touch you
- You decide when it's okay to be hugged or held
- You decide how you want to say no

Even if someone is older, or in your family, or a teacher—if it feels wrong or weird, you must listen to that feeling.

Public vs Private Parts of the Body

Let's talk about something really important.
Our bodies have many parts. Some are public, and some are private.

- **Public Parts:** These include your arms, legs, head, hands, and feet.
- **Private Parts:** These are the areas covered by a swimsuit—your chest, bottom, and the area between your legs.

Private parts are private for a reason.

Rule: No one should look at, touch, or ask to see your private parts.

The only time it is okay is:

- If a doctor is checking you with your parent present
- If your parent is helping you clean or change and you are okay with it

If someone touches you in a way that feels wrong or tells you "Don't tell anyone"—that is a big red flag.
Always tell a trusted adult.

What Is Safe Touch and Unsafe Touch?

We can also understand touch in two ways:
Safe Touch

- A hug from your parent when you're upset
- A high five from a friend

• A nurse giving you a vaccine
These make you feel cared for, respected, and safe.

Unsafe Touch
• Someone tickling you when you've said stop
• Someone touching you in private areas
• Someone making you feel uncomfortable and saying, "Don't tell anyone"
These make you feel scared, confused, or uncomfortable.
Always remember: If the touch feels bad—it is bad.

Try It

Let's play a few learning games!

Game: Safe or Unsafe?

Say "Safe" or "Unsafe" for each situation:
1. Your mother helps you apply medicine on a wound.
2. A classmate touches your chest and laughs.
3. A teacher pats your shoulder for good work.
4. An uncle tickles you and doesn't stop when you ask.
5. A friend holds your hand while crossing the road.

Answers:
1. Safe
2. Unsafe
3. Safe
4. Unsafe
5. Safe

Practice Saying "No"

Stand in front of a mirror and practice saying:
• "I don't like that."
• "No! Please stop."

• "That's not okay."
• "I will tell someone I trust."
Use a strong, confident voice. Not angry, but not soft either. Just firm and clear.

Think & Reflect

• Have you ever felt uncomfortable with someone's touch but stayed quiet? Why?
• Who are the adults you trust at home and school?
• Why do you think it's important to speak up?
• Is it okay to say "no" to grown-ups?

Let's Revise

Let's remember the golden rules of body safety:
✔ You are the boss of your body
✔ You can say "NO" to any touch that feels wrong
✔ Private parts must be protected
✔ Unsafe touch should never be kept a secret
✔ Always tell a trusted adult
✔ Use your voice and body to stay safe

Check Yourself

Multiple Choice Questions:

1. What should you do if someone touches you in a way that feels wrong?
    - Stay silent
    - Blame yourself
    - Tell a trusted adult immediately ✔

2. What are private parts?
    - Hands and feet
    - Shoulders and head
    - Parts covered by a swimsuit ✔

3. Who can help clean your private parts when needed?
    - Any adult
    - Parent or doctor with your permission ✔
    - A classmate

True or False:

4. It's wrong to say no to a teacher. **False**
5. You should keep unsafe touch a secret. **False**
6. Your body belongs to you. **True**
7. Unsafe touch can make you feel scared or confused. **True**

Creative Task:

Draw a poster titled "My Body, My Rules".

Include:

- Safe vs unsafe touch examples
- 3 trusted adults
- Body safety slogans like "I am brave" or "No Means No"

Beyond the Book

Activity: "Safety Flower"

Draw a flower with 5 petals. On each petal,

write:

- One person I can trust
- One way to say no
- One safe place
- One safety rule
- One good secret and one bad secret

Discuss the difference:

- Good secrets are about birthdays or surprises
- Bad secrets are about hurt or unsafe touch and must be shared

Family Safety Talk

Ask your parents:

• "What should I do if someone makes me uncomfortable?"

• "Who are three people I can go to for help?"

Write down the answers in your notebook.

Words to Learn (Glossary)

Word	Meaning
Trusted Adult	A grown-up you can talk to when scared
Private Parts	Body areas covered by swimsuit
Unsafe Touch	A touch that feels scary, wrong, or confusing
Safe Touch	A touch that feels caring and respectful
Boundaries	Personal rules about your body

Real Life Story: Aarav's Brave Voice

Aarav, age 9, was in a lift when a stranger leaned too close and asked, "What's your name, little boy?" Aarav felt nervous. He remembered his safety rule—if it feels wrong, get out.

He quickly pressed the next floor, got off the lift, and ran to his building guard.

Later, he told his parents, who praised him for his smart thinking. Self-defence is not just about strength. It's about knowing what's right and doing it.

Chapter 3

Awareness is Your First Shield

It was the end of the school day. Aarush and his friend Divya were walking home. While crossing the street, Divya noticed a car parked nearby with someone inside staring at them. Aarush was busy playing a mobile game. Divya pulled his hand and said, “Let’s go around the other way.” Aarush frowned but followed her. Later, the car drove away.

“Why did we take the longer route?” he asked.

“Because that man gave me a weird feeling. It didn’t seem safe,” Divya replied. That moment saved them from possible danger. And guess what helped? Awareness.

Explore

What Is Awareness?

Awareness means being alert, watching, listening, and understanding what is happening around you. It is your first line of defence—even before running, yelling, or saying “No!”

Imagine your brain is like a superhero radar. It scans your

surroundings and tells you:

- Is this place safe?
- Who is around me?
- What sounds do I hear?
- Is someone following me?
- Should I stay or move away?

When you're aware, you can stop trouble before it starts.

Why Awareness Matters

Did you know that most unsafe situations can be avoided just by being alert?

Here's why awareness is so important:

- It helps you sense danger early
- You can take action before things get worse
- It builds your confidence
- It keeps your mind calm
- It makes others think twice before troubling you

Think of awareness like a shield—the stronger it is, the harder it is for danger to reach you.

Where to Use Awareness

You can use your awareness everywhere. Here are some common situations:

While Travelling

- Be aware of who gets on or off the bus
- Avoid sitting alone in the back if it's empty
- Keep your school bag close
- Never talk to strangers or take things from them

In School

- Notice who walks behind you in corridors

• Stay alert in washrooms or staircases
• Be careful if someone tries to block your way or touch your things

In the Neighbourhood
• Avoid dark, empty streets when alone
• Always walk where there are people
• Inform parents if you see something suspicious

Online
Yes, awareness is needed even on the internet!
• Don't click links from strangers
• Never share photos or personal details
• If someone makes you uncomfortable in a game or chat, tell an adult

Try It

Activity: Awareness Check
Next time you go to the park or school

Try this:
1. Look around. Who do you see?
2. Listen carefully. What sounds do you hear?
3. Notice your path. Are there quiet corners or dark spots?
4. Count your steps. How far is the nearest adult or help point?
Write or draw your findings in a "Safety Notebook."

5-Second Scan Game
Every time you enter a new space (room, class, bus, shop)

take 5 seconds to:
• Scan the people
• Find exits
• Spot cameras or helpers
• Notice anything odd

Practice this daily and you'll build a strong awareness habit.

Safety Senses: Trusting Your Gut

Sometimes, your body feels something is wrong—even before you know why.
This is called your instinct or gut feeling.

It might feel like:
• A heavy chest
• Fast heartbeat
• Sweaty palms
• Wanting to leave

Never ignore this feeling. If it feels wrong, it probably is.

Think & Reflect

• Have you ever had a bad gut feeling? What did you do?
• How can being alert stop a bad situation from happening?
• Do you think being aware makes you look more confident?
• What would you do if someone tried to secretly follow you?

Let's Revise

Let's put all our learning into simple points:
✔ Awareness means being alert and watching your surroundings
✔ It is your first shield—even before using your voice or body
✔ Use all 5 senses—see, hear, feel, smell, and even your gut
✔ Pay attention in public, at school, at home, and online
✔ If something feels wrong, act immediately—move away or tell someone

Check Yourself

Multiple Choice Questions:

1. What does "awareness" mean in self-defence?
   - Sleeping peacefully
   - Noticing your surroundings ✔
   - Running fast

2. When should you scan your surroundings?
   - Only when you're scared
   - Whenever you enter a new space ✔
   - Only at school

3. What does your "gut feeling" help with?
   - Telling jokes
   - Warning you about danger ✔
   - Finding your friend's house

True or False:

4. You should trust your gut if something feels off. **True**
5. Awareness is only needed for grown-ups. **False**
6. Looking confident makes people think twice before troubling you. **True**
7. You don't need awareness while using the internet. **False**

Creative Corner:

Draw yourself as a Safety Detective with a magnifying glass. Around the drawing,

write or illustrate:

- "What I see"
- "What I hear"
- "What I feel"
- "What I do when it feels unsafe"

Beyond the Book

Create Your "Awareness Diary"

Each day for one week, write 3 things you observed during your travel to school:
1. Who was near you?
2. Did anything make you uncomfortable?
3. What did you do about it?

Review your notes with a parent or teacher.

Map It Out

With your teacher or parent, draw a map of your school or neighbourhood.

Mark:
- Safe spaces (staff room, friend's house, shop)
- Unsafe corners (empty rooms, alley, broken lights)
- Help points (security guards, police booth)

Stick this map in your safety file.

Real Life Story: Vedika's Smart Eyes

Vedika, 10, was returning from tuitions. She saw a man sitting on a scooter near the gate. Something felt odd—he wasn't using his phone or moving. Vedika remembered her "Awareness Rule" and turned around to walk home through a crowded lane. She later told her mother, who thanked her for being so alert.

Moral: Awareness can stop trouble before it begins.

Words to Learn (Glossary)

Word	Meaning
Awareness	Noticing what's around you using your senses
Instinct	A strong feeling that something is right or wrong
Surroundings	The people, places, and things around you
Alert	Ready to notice and respond to danger
Safe Space	A place where you feel protected and calm

Chapter 4

Using Your Voice – Loud and Clear!

Ritu was at her school canteen. A boy from the senior class came and kept standing too close to her. He whispered, "Come with me, or I'll tell everyone your secret." Ritu felt scared for a moment, but then she remembered something her teacher had said during a self-defence workshop:

"Your voice is your first and strongest weapon."

Ritu stood tall, looked straight at him, and said loudly, "Leave me alone!" Everyone turned. The boy backed off. A teacher came over. Ritu felt safe again. Just like Ritu, you can learn to use your voice as a powerful tool to protect yourself.

Explore

Why Is Your Voice So Powerful?

You may think self-defence means physical strength. But guess what? Your voice is your first line of defence. It's always with you, it's free to use, and it can stop bad behaviour before it becomes dangerous.

Your voice helps you:

- Speak up when something feels wrong
- Get attention from people nearby
- Set boundaries ("Stop! That's not okay!")
- Scare off someone who is trying to hurt or scare you
- Show that you are not a quiet or easy target

"A strong voice can break silence, fear, and danger."

When Should You Use Your Voice?

You don't need to shout all the time. But in self-defence, using your voice in the right moment can protect you.

Speak Up When:

- Someone touches you in a way you don't like
- Someone says mean or threatening things
- A person tries to take you somewhere without permission
- You feel unsafe or unsure
- You see someone else being bullied

Say It Loud, Say It Clear:

- "No!"
- "Stop!"
- "I don't like that!"
- "Leave me alone!"
- "Help me!"
- "That's not okay!"

You don't have to scream like in a movie—but your tone should be firm, loud enough, and confident.

Voice Types and When to Use Them

Voice Type	When to Use	Example
Calm Voice	Asking for help politely	"Excuse me, I need help."
Strong Voice	Setting boundaries	"Stop it. That's not okay."
Loud Voice	To alert others in danger	"Help! I need help!"
Authority Voice	When you need to take control	"Back off now!"

Pro Tip: Practice switching between voice types. Your tone matters as much as the words you say.

Try It

Voice Practice Game

With a parent or teacher, practice saying these sentences:
1. Say "No" like you mean it!
2. Say "Help!" like you're in trouble.
3. Say "I don't like that" with confidence.
4. Say "Leave me alone" in a strong tone.

Repeat each sentence three times—first softly, then firmly, and finally loudly. Which one felt most powerful?

Role Play: The Power of Voice

Act out these situations and respond with your voice:
- Someone grabs your arm at the park
- A friend dares you to go into a stranger's house
- A stranger offers you a ride in a car

• Someone tries to take your bag at the bus stop

How did it feel to speak up? Did your voice change how the scene ended?

The Science Behind It

Did you know?

When you speak confidently, people:
• Take you more seriously
• Are less likely to pick on you
• Step back and give you space
• Are more willing to help you

Your voice sends a message that you are alert, aware, and ready to protect yourself. Bullies and strangers often leave confident kids alone.

Think & Reflect

• Have you ever been too scared to speak up? Why?
• What would happen if you didn't say anything in a risky situation?
• Who in your life has a strong voice? What makes it strong?
• Can your voice help others too? How?

Let's Revise

Let's lock in what we've learned about using your voice:
✔ Your voice is your first and fastest self-defence tool
✔ Use it to say NO, call for help, and set boundaries
✔ Practice using your voice in different situations
✔ Speak clearly, firmly, and with confidence
✔ If someone is being bullied or hurt—speak up for them too!

Check Yourself

Multiple Choice Questions:

1. What is your voice used for in self-defence?
    - Singing songs
    - Saying "No" and calling for help ✔
    - Whispering to your friend

2. What kind of voice should you use in danger?
    - Very soft
    - Loud and confident ✔
    - Laughing voice

3. Which sentence is best for setting boundaries?
    - "I guess that's okay..."
    - "Stop! I don't like that." ✔
    - "Let's play later."

True or False:

4. Using your voice makes you look confident. **True**
5. Bullies like kids who speak up. **False**
6. You can use your voice to help others too. **True**
7. Shouting is always the best choice. **False**

Creative Corner:

Write and decorate your personal "Power Phrases Poster" **with these:**

- "No means no!"
- "Stop that right now!"
- "I will tell a trusted adult."
- "My voice is strong!"
- "I can speak up!"

Put it on your room wall or school bag as a reminder.

Beyond the Book

Voice Journal
For one week, write in a diary each time you:
- Spoke up when something didn't feel right
- Helped a friend by using your voice
- Practiced your "NO!" voice at home

Reflect:
Did it feel easy or hard to speak up?

Family Voice Practice

Invite your family members to take part in:
- Saying safety phrases in strong voices
- Playing the "Voice Switch" game (soft, firm, loud)
- Practicing what to say during emergencies

Real-Life Story: Sahil Stood Up

Sahil was being teased on the school bus. At first, he stayed quiet.
But the jokes continued.
One day, he stood up and said,
"This is not funny. Please stop."
He said it clearly in front of everyone.
The bullies were shocked and left him alone.
The next day, one of his friends said,
"Sahil, I admire your courage."

Courage doesn't always roar. Sometimes, it's the voice that says, 'No more!'

Words to Learn (Glossary)

Word	Meaning
Boundary	A rule that protects your personal space or feelings
Confident	Feeling strong and sure of yourself
Tone	The sound and feeling in your voice
Assertive	Speaking firmly without being rude
Authority	A voice or action that shows control and leadership

Chapter 5

Hands Up! Defensive Postures

Yuvraj was walking to his karate class when a group of older boys stopped him. One of them stepped forward, pretending to joke around, but tried to grab his backpack. Yuvraj didn't panic. He remembered his self-defence training. He raised his hands—not to hit, but to protect. His hands were open, his feet apart, and his knees slightly bent. "Don't touch me!" he said, loud and clear. The boys laughed, but they stepped back. They weren't expecting a child to look so alert, ready, and confident. Yuvraj didn't have to hit anyone. Just his defensive posture was enough.

This chapter will teach you what Yuvraj knew—how to use your body posture to defend without fighting.

Explore

What Is a Defensive Posture?
A defensive posture means the way you hold your body, hands, feet, and head when you feel unsafe.

It helps you:

- Show confidence
- Protect your face and body
- Create space between you and the threat
- Prepare to move, block, or call for help

You don't need to know karate to have a defensive posture. It's something everyone can learn.

Defensive postures are peaceful, strong, and smart. They protect you and help avoid conflict.

The "Hands Up" Position

The most basic defensive posture is "Hands Up." It's simple and powerful.

How to Do It:

1. Stand with your feet shoulder-width apart
2. Bend your knees slightly—like you're ready to move
3. Raise your hands to shoulder height
4. Keep your palms open and facing the other person
5. Keep your elbows bent and your hands near your cheeks

This posture looks non-threatening,

but it:

- Protects your face and head
- Lets you push away or block if needed
- Shows others you are alert and not an easy target

"Hands up" doesn't mean you want to fight—it shows you are ready to protect.

Defensive Foot Position

Your feet are just as important as your hands.

Try This:
- Place one foot a little in front of the other
- Keep both feet firmly on the ground
- Don't stand stiff—stay balanced and relaxed
- Keep your weight in the middle so you can move quickly

This stance helps you stay stable and ready to act if needed.

Why Posture Matters

Posture isn't just about your body. It sends a message to the world. **When you stand straight, hands up, and eyes alert, you tell others:**
- "I'm aware of what's going on."
- "I'm not going to be an easy target."
- "I'm ready to protect myself."

Bullies often choose people who look nervous, quiet, or unsure. A confident posture can scare off trouble before it begins.

Try It

Practice the "Hands Up" Drill

1. Stand in front of a mirror
2. Get into your Hands Up posture
3. **Practice saying these lines:**
   - o "I don't want trouble."
   - o "Stay away from me."
   - o "I'm asking you to stop."

Do it five times. How do you look? Strong? Calm? Ready?

Role Play Scenarios

Act out the following scenes with a friend, sibling, or parent:
1. Someone is standing too close to you in line
2. A stranger grabs your hand
3. A bully is trying to block your path
Use your defensive posture and voice. What changes when you raise your hands and take a strong stance?

Add Facial Awareness

Even your face matters in a defensive posture!
• Keep your eyes open
• Don't look down or away—make eye contact
• Don't smile if you feel unsafe
• Look serious, calm, and firm

Your face, eyes, and body should all say: "I don't want to fight, but I'm not afraid."

Bonus Move: The "Step-Back Block"

Want a simple move that even kids can use? Try this:
1. Start in "Hands Up" posture
2. If someone tries to touch you, take one step back
3. Use your front arm to gently block or push their hand away
4. Say, "Stop. Do not touch me."

This move creates space and lets you prepare to move, yell, or run.

Think & Reflect

• When was the last time your body language helped you?
• Do you usually stand straight or slouch? Why?
• How can your posture stop bullying or unsafe behaviour?

• Have you ever felt unsafe but didn't know how to respond with your body?

Let's Revise

Here are the big lessons of this chapter:

✔ A defensive posture helps protect you from danger

✔ "Hands Up" is simple but powerful—open palms, elbows bent, feet firm

✔ Stand straight, alert, and balanced

✔ Eye contact and a serious face make you look confident

✔ You can create space and prepare to run or shout if needed

Check Yourself

Multiple Choice Questions:

1. What does a defensive posture help with?
    - Fighting someone
    - Protecting yourself ✔
    - Sleeping better

2. In the "Hands Up" posture, your palms should face:
    - Your pockets
    - The person in front of you ✔
    - The sky

3. What should your feet do in a defensive stance?
    - Stand very close together
    - Stay apart and balanced ✔
    - Keep moving in circles

True or False:

4. Posture shows how confident you are. **True**
5. It's okay to smile when someone threatens you. **False**
6. You should look down when you feel unsafe. **False**

7. “Hands Up” is used to scare people. **False**
8. A step-back block can help you create space. **True**

Creative Corner:

Draw your superhero version of yourself in “Hands Up” posture.

Add speech bubbles like:

- “I’m ready to protect myself.”
- “Back off, please.”
- “I said no!”

Beyond the Book

Posture Challenge

Every morning for one week, stand in front of a mirror for one minute:

- Stand tall
- Raise your hands in defence
- Say a power phrase (e.g., “I am strong. I am aware. I am safe.”)

Rate how confident you feel from 1–10. Watch the score go up every day!

Group Game: “Freeze and Pose”

With your class or friends, play music. When it stops, shout “Danger!”

Everyone freezes into a defensive posture. The best and calmest posture wins!

Real-Life Story: Khushi’s Smart Stance

Khushi, age 11, was at a shopping mall when a stranger asked her to come help find a lost phone. She felt nervous. She didn’t move. Instead, she stepped back, raised her hands, and said, “Don’t come near me.”

A nearby shopkeeper heard and came to help. The stranger ran away. Khushi didn’t need to fight. Her stance and voice said everything.

Words to Learn (Glossary)

Word	Meaning
Posture	The way you hold your body when standing or sitting
Defensive	Meant to protect, not attack
Stance	How you place your feet and legs
Awareness	Being alert and ready
Block	A way to stop or deflect contact

Chapter 6

Simple Moves for Big Safety

Imagine this:

Karan was on his way back from school. A man on a bike tried to grab his bag and pull him. Karan didn't panic. He remembered what his self-defence instructor had said—"Small moves can save big problems." He turned sideways, held his bag tight, kicked backward with his foot, and shouted, "Help!" loudly. The man lost balance and ran off.

Karan didn't punch or do any fancy moves. He just used some simple, smart actions that he had practiced. These small moves helped him stay safe.

In this chapter, you'll learn easy, practical self-defence techniques that you can use anytime, anywhere. No need for black belts—just some practice, awareness, and confidence!

Explore

Why Learn Physical Self-Defence Moves?

So far, you've learned that the best self-defence begins in the mind—

with awareness, confidence, voice, and posture. But sometimes, the danger is close, and you need to use your body to protect yourself. You're not learning to fight.

You're learning how to:

- Escape from a grab
- Create space to run away
- Block a harmful move
- Use simple motions that surprise or distract the attacker
- Stay calm and in control of your own body

"You don't need to fight to be safe—you need to think fast and move smart."

Simple, Safe, Smart Moves for Kids

Let's look at basic self-defence techniques that are safe, effective, and easy to practice.

1. Knee Strike

When to use:

If someone is very close and trying to grab you or pick you up.

How to do it:

1. Raise one knee high
2. Drive it upward and forward
3. Aim for their thighs, stomach, or groin
4. Yell "NO!" loudly while doing it

Tip: Do this only if you cannot escape. The goal is to surprise them and run.

2. Heel Stomp

When to use:

If someone grabs you from behind or stands too close.

How to do it:
1. Raise your heel slightly
2. Stomp down hard on their foot
3. Turn sideways and run

Tip: The top of the foot is very sensitive. This move is great to break free.

3. Palm Strike
When to use:
If someone's hand is reaching toward your face or chest.

How to do it:
1. Keep your fingers together and hand open
2. Push your palm straight out
3. Aim for their chin, chest, or nose
4. Shout while doing it

Tip: Keep your elbow slightly bent and don't slap—use the base of your palm.

4. Arm Block
When to use:
If someone tries to grab your arm or wrist.

How to do it:
1. Bend your other arm in an "L" shape
2. Sweep it across to push their hand off
3. Step back and get into your "Hands Up" position
4. Say "Let go!" or "Don't touch me!"

Tip: Twist your wrist gently as you pull away to break their grip.

5. The Twist and Run
When to use:

If someone grabs your arm or shoulder.

How to do it:
1. Step to the side
2. Twist your body quickly
3. Pull your arm back
4. Turn and run as fast as you can

Tip: The faster the twist, the easier it is to escape. Don't wait—run!

Try It

Here are some practice games and partner drills you can do at home or school (under adult supervision).
Grab and Escape Game

One person gently grabs your wrist.
Try different methods to:
- Twist out of it
- Block with the other hand
- Shout while moving back

Switch roles. Talk about which moves felt easy or strong.

Shadow Defence Drill
Stand in front of a mirror. Practice:
- Knee strikes
- Palm pushes
- Arm blocks
- Heel stomps

Do them slowly, then with more energy. Add a power phrase each time:
- "Back off!"
- "Don't touch me!"
- "I said no!"

Safety First!

While practicing:

- Always use soft touches
- Never aim for someone's eyes or face
- Respect your partner's space
- Wear comfortable clothes
- Practice on mats or soft ground if possible

Self-defence is for protection, not for showing off or hurting friends.

Think & Reflect

- Which move do you think you can use if grabbed from behind?
- Have you ever felt stuck in a situation where movement could help?
- Why is it better to escape than to fight?
- Can you teach someone younger these moves safely?

Let's Revise

Key takeaways from this chapter:

✔ Self-defence moves should be simple, quick, and smart
✔ Use your knees, feet, palms, and elbows
✔ Always yell while defending—it attracts help
✔ Practice regularly to build muscle memory
✔ Defend only to escape, not to fight

Check Yourself

Multiple Choice Questions:

1. What is the purpose of self-defence moves?
    - To show off strength
    - To protect and escape from danger ✔
    - To fight with others

2. What should you say while using a move?
    - Say nothing
    - Shout "No!" or "Stop!" ✔
    - Apologize

3. Which part of the body is used in a heel stomp?
    - Hand
    - Shoulder
    - Foot ✔

True or False:

4. Self-defence moves should be used to hurt the attacker. **False**
5. You should never practice moves without an adult's guidance. **True**
6. A palm strike is done with a closed fist. **False**
7. Your goal should be to create space and run. **True**

Creative Corner:

Draw stick figures showing:

- A knee strike
- A heel stomp
- An arm block

Label each with when to use it.

Beyond the Book

Safety Move Challenge
Make flashcards with different danger scenes. Shuffle and pick one. Now act out the best self-defence move for that situation. Do this with family or friends as a fun game!

Record and Reflect
Ask your parent or teacher to record you practicing three moves.

Watch it later and answer:

- Did I stand strong?
- Did I yell clearly?
- Was I fast and focused?

Try again the next day—track your improvement.

Real-Life Story: Navya's Move That Saved Her

Navya, 10, was walking to the store when someone on a scooter stopped and reached for her hand. Navya remembered her training. She stepped back, stomped on his foot, twisted away, and shouted, "Help!" loud enough for people to gather. The man fled.

Small move. Big result. Smart kid.

Words to Learn (Glossary)

Word	Meaning
Technique	A way to do something, like a move or step
Stomp	To hit the ground with your foot hard
Block	A move that stops someone from touching you
Strike	A strong action with a body part (like palm or knee)
Escape	To get away from danger or trouble

Chapter 7

Staying Safe with Friends and Family

Aarav loved going to play at his cousin's house. One evening, while playing video games, his older cousin started showing him strange pictures on the phone. Aarav felt confused and uncomfortable. He wanted to leave but didn't want to "be rude." Later, he told his mother what happened.

She hugged him and said, "Thank you for telling me. You always have the right to feel safe—even with family."

In this chapter, we will learn how to stay safe with friends, relatives, and familiar people—the ones we often trust the most.

Explore

Do You Know?

Most people think that danger comes from strangers. But research and real-life cases show that many unsafe situations for children happen with people they already know—a family friend, neighbour, relative, cousin, or even a classmate.

But don't worry!

This chapter will help you:

- Recognize uncomfortable or tricky situations
- Speak up when you feel unsafe—even if it's someone close
- Set boundaries in friendships and family
- Understand the difference between love and control

"Safe relationships make you feel happy, not scared or confused."

What Does "Safe With Known People" Mean?

It means being comfortable, respected, and in control—even when you're with people you know and care about.

A person who loves and respects you will:

- Ask before touching you
- Accept your "No"
- Never keep secrets from your parents
- Never threaten, bribe, or pressure you
- Encourage you to tell the truth

If someone makes you feel bad, scared, or uncomfortable—even a little—you have the right to walk away, say no, and tell someone you trust.

Examples of Tricky Situations

Here are some situations that may feel confusing:

Situation	Safe or Unsafe?	What You Can Do
A friend keeps hugging you even when you say no	Unsafe	Say "Stop", step away, and tell an adult
A cousin shares scary or rude videos	Unsafe	Leave the room, tell a parent

Your uncle says "Don't tell anyone" after giving you a weird gift	Unsafe	Tell your trusted adult
A friend dares you to steal candy and says, "If you don't, I'll tell your secret"	Unsafe	Refuse, and tell a teacher
Your aunt helps you change clothes for swimming and asks questions about your body	Unsafe	Say "I can do it myself," and talk to your parents

Rule: If someone says "Don't tell anyone," it's usually a sign to tell someone immediately.

Safety in Friendships

Friends are important. They help us feel happy, supported, and included. But even friends can sometimes do things that are not okay.

Signs of a safe friend:
- Listens to your feelings
- Respects your choices
- Doesn't force or dare you to do things
- Apologizes when they hurt you
- Makes you feel good about yourself

Signs of an unsafe friend:
- Always wants things their way
- Laughs when you're hurt or upset
- Asks for your secrets or passwords
- Tries to make you hide things from adults

• Touches you in ways that make you uncomfortable

You have the right to leave, take a break, or talk to an adult if your friendship feels unsafe.

Try It

Think-Pair-Share

Work with a classmate or parent. For each statement, say:
• Safe
• Unsafe
• Ask for Help
1. Your best friend asks for your school ID password
2. Your cousin says they'll only play with you if you don't tell your mom what you did
3. Your aunt always hugs you without asking
4. Your classmate helps you when you're sad
5. Your older sibling locks the door and tells you to play a secret game

Discuss your answers. Remember, your feelings are the best clues.

Role Play: Saying "No" to Friends or Family

Practice these scenes with your teacher, sibling, or friend:
1. Someone tickles you even after you ask them to stop
2. Your cousin wants to see your private pictures
3. A classmate tells you not to sit with your other friends
4. A friend dares you to lie to your parents

Practice saying:
• "I don't want to."
• "That makes me uncomfortable."
• "I'm telling my parents."

• "No, thank you."
Say it clearly, with confidence, but politely.

Think & Reflect

• Have you ever felt unsafe with someone you knew? What did you do?
• Why is it harder to say "No" to people you know?
• Can a good friend or family member sometimes make a mistake?
• How can you tell the difference between a safe and unsafe touch—even from someone close?

Let's Revise

Let's remember these safety basics:
✔ You have the right to say "No" to anyone—even friends or family
✔ Safe people respect your space, voice, and feelings
✔ If someone says, "Keep this a secret from your parents," tell your parents immediately
✔ Tricky people are not always strangers—they can be people you know
✔ You can walk away, speak up, and get help anytime

Check Yourself

Multiple Choice Questions:

1. What should you do if a cousin shows you inappropriate pictures?
    - Stay quiet
    - Leave and tell a trusted adult ✔
    - Show your friends

2. A good friend will:
    - Take your personal things
    - Make you feel scared
    - Respect your boundaries ✔

3. What is a "tricky person"?
   - Someone who plays magic tricks
   - Someone who tries to confuse you or break rules secretly ✔
   - A silly clown

True or False:

4. It's okay to say "No" to a family member. **True**
5. Friends can never do anything wrong. **False**
6. Secrets that make you feel scared should be told to adults. **True**
7. You must hug your relatives even if you don't want to. **False**

Creative Corner:
Make a poster titled:
"I Can Be Safe with People I Know"

Add drawings of:
- Red flags (e.g., secrets, unsafe touch)
- Green flags (e.g., kind, respectful, honest)
- Your trusted adults list

Beyond the Book

Home Activity: Safety Tree
Create a "Safety Tree" with:
- The trunk = You
- Branches = People you know
- Green leaves = People who make you feel safe
- Red leaves = People who make you feel unsure

Share it with your parents and discuss how you feel.

Make a "Trust Card"
Write down:
- 3 adults you trust
- Their phone numbers
- What you can talk to them about (e.g., secrets, safety, feelings)

Keep this card in your schoolbag or diary.

Real-Life Story: Ishaan Speaks Up

Ishaan loved his uncle's visits. But one day, the uncle tickled him too much, and Ishaan asked him to stop. He didn't. Ishaan felt trapped. Later, he told his mom, who believed him immediately.
She spoke to the uncle, and Ishaan never had to be around him again.

Ishaan didn't fight. He didn't run. He spoke up, and that made all the difference.

Words to Learn (Glossary)

Word	Meaning
Boundary	A line that tells what's okay and what's not
Tricky Person	Someone who tries to confuse or hide wrong things
Unsafe Touch	A touch that makes you feel bad or scared
Respect	To listen, care, and honour someone's space or choice
Secret	Something hidden—but not all secrets should be kept

Chapter 8

Online Safety – Defending in Digital Spaces

Tanvi loved playing online games. One day, she got a friend request from someone named "CoolBoy_99." He seemed nice and sent her gifts in the game. But soon, he started asking for personal details—her photo, school name, and mobile number. Tanvi felt nervous. She stopped replying and told her parents.

Together, they reported the user and deleted the game. Tanvi stayed safe because she used her online self-defence skills.

In this chapter, you'll learn how to protect yourself in the digital world just like you do in the real world—using your mind, voice, and good choices.

Explore

What Is Online Safety?

Online safety means using the internet, apps, and digital tools in a way that keeps you:

- Protected from strangers
- Safe from bullying

• In control of your information
• Happy and confident while learning or playing

The internet is like a giant playground—fun and useful, but also filled with people you don't know. Just like you wouldn't talk to a stranger in a park, you should also be careful online.

"If it feels wrong online, it probably is."

Where Do You Need Online Safety?

You must practice digital self-defence when you:
• Use apps or games
• Watch videos or cartoons
• Chat with friends
• Attend online classes
• Use a mobile, tablet, or computer
• Share photos, drawings, or projects online

10 Golden Rules of Online Safety

Here are ten must-know tips to keep yourself protected:

1. Never share personal info online
✗ Full name, address, school name, photos, passwords
✔ Use nicknames and never post your real details

2. Only talk to people you know
Don't accept friend requests from strangers—even if they seem kind

3. Don't post photos without permission
That includes selfies, school pictures, or family moments

4. Say NO to bullying
If someone makes fun of you online, don't reply—report and block

5. Use strong passwords
Mix letters, numbers, and symbols. Change them regularly.

6. Ask before downloading
Some games and apps may have viruses or bad content

7. Keep screen time limited
Long screen hours can hurt your eyes, health, and sleep

8. Always log out
After school classes or games, log out so no one misuses your account

9. If you feel uncomfortable, stop immediately
Tell a parent or trusted adult

10. Remember: Not everything online is true
Think twice before believing, sharing, or reacting

Try It

Online Safety Quiz Game

Decide if each is Safe or Unsafe:

1. Using your school name as your game username
2. Playing a game where someone asks to meet in real life
3. Using a password like "12345"
4. Watching videos from your school's learning portal
5. Posting a dance video online with your home in the background

Answers:

1. Unsafe
2. Unsafe
3. Unsafe
4. Safe
5. Unsafe

Tech Talk with Family

Ask your parents:

- What apps are okay for me to use?
- Can I create a game account with your help?
- What do I do if someone asks for my phone number online?

Write the answers in your Digital Safety Diary.

What Is Cyberbullying?

Cyberbullying is when someone:

- Sends you mean messages
- Posts rude comments
- Shares your private photos or info
- Spreads lies about you online
- Excludes you from chats or groups on purpose

Bullying is never okay—online or offline.
Always speak up, block the bully, and tell a trusted adult.

What Are Safe vs Unsafe Websites?

Safe Sites	**Unsafe Sites**
School learning portals	Random gaming or video download sites
Government educational apps	Sites with pop-up ads and strange links
Family YouTube channels	Channels with violence or hate speech
Child-safe browsers	Sites that ask for personal data or payments

Tip: Ask your teacher or parent before visiting a new site.

Cyber Smart Moves

Be a Cyber Smart Kid by doing the following:

- Use a password manager (ask your parent to set it up)
- Use child-safe browsers like YouTube Kids
- Turn off location sharing on your devices
- Keep your camera covered when not in use
- Report strangers or bullies using the report or block button
- Install an antivirus app on your device

Remember: "Click with care."

Think & Reflect

- Have you ever shared something online and regretted it?
- Do you know anyone who faced bullying on a game or app?
- What would you do if someone you trust sent you something that felt wrong?
- Why is logging out after class or gaming important?

Let's Revise

Here's a recap of what you've learned:

✔ The internet is fun but needs rules and awareness
✔ Don't share personal info—keep it private
✔ Only talk to people you know
✔ Say no to bullying and unsafe messages
✔ Use strong passwords and log out every time
✔ Ask adults before downloading anything
✔ If something feels off, stop and tell
✔ Not everything online is true—think before you believe

Check Yourself

Multiple Choice Questions:

1. What should you do if someone sends you a bad message online?
   - Reply and shout at them
   - Ignore and keep quiet
   - Report and tell a trusted adult ✔

2. Why should you not share your photo online?
   - Because it's boring
   - Because strangers can misuse it ✔
   - Because no one will like it

3. What is a strong password?
   - MyName123
   - A mix of letters, numbers, symbols ✔
   - Password123

True or False:

4. It's okay to chat with strangers in an online game. **False**
5. You should tell your parents before installing an app. **True**
6. Cyberbullying only happens to grown-ups. **False**
7. Logging out protects your account. **True**

Creative Corner:
Design a poster:
"My 5 Online Safety Rules"
Use colourful symbols like locks, red flags, stop signs, and computers.

Beyond the Book

Build a Digital Safety Plan
With your parent or teacher:

• List the apps and games you use
• Set screen time rules
• Create backup passwords
• Keep emergency contacts handy
Stick this plan near your study desk.

School Cyber Pledge
Say it aloud and share with your classmates:
"I will stay smart, safe, and kind online.
I will protect my info and report anything wrong.
I will not be a bully or share things that hurt others."
Print it, sign it, and keep it in your school diary.

Real-Life Story: Tanish's Online Trouble

Tanish loved Minecraft. One day, someone in his game group asked for his photo and said he'd get free rewards. Tanish almost sent it but felt unsure. He told his dad instead.
They blocked the user, reported it, and talked about online rules.

One smart choice made all the difference.

Words to Learn (Glossary)

Word	Meaning
Cyberbullying	Bullying that happens through phones, games, or internet
Privacy	Keeping personal info safe and hidden
Stranger	Someone you don't know in real life
Report	Telling the app or adults about a problem online
Password	A secret word or code used to protect your account

Chapter 9

Safe in Public – Travel, Parks, and Streets

Naira was walking to her tuition class when she noticed a man following her for two blocks. She remembered what her teacher had taught: "When in public, stay alert, don't panic, and trust your gut." Naira walked quickly to a nearby shop, told the shopkeeper what happened, and asked to call her mother. She stayed safe that day. Whether it's a crowded market or a quiet lane, children must know how to protect themselves in public spaces. This chapter will help you stay smart, alert, and safe when you're outside your home.

Explore

Why Public Safety Matters
Public places—like parks, streets, shops, buses, and even lifts—are not always dangerous.

But sometimes, unexpected things happen:
• Someone may follow or stare at you
• You may feel lost or stuck

• A stranger might ask you for help
• You might get separated from your parents
• Someone may try to grab your bag or touch you inappropriately
Learning public safety is about being prepared, not scared.

"The more aware you are, the more control you have."

Common Public Spaces Where You Need Awareness

Place	Possible Risks	Safety Tip
Roads & streets	Being followed, traffic	Walk on the side, avoid shortcuts
Bus stands	Crowds, strangers	Wait in safe, well-lit areas
Parks	Getting lost, bullying	Stay with friends or trusted adults
Markets & malls	Separation from guardians	Know a meeting point and contact
Elevators	Getting trapped with strangers	Enter only if it feels safe

10 Street-Smart Safety Rules

1. **Walk with confidence**
   Head high, eyes alert, shoulders back—don't look lost or nervous.

2. **Stick to busy and well-lit paths**
   Avoid dark alleys, isolated parks, or shortcut routes—especially alone.

3. **Stay alert—no distractions**
   No headphones, loud music, or games while walking alone.

4. **Trust your instincts**
   If something feels wrong, change direction, go into a shop, or ask for help.

5. **Keep emergency numbers ready**
   Save parents' numbers and know local help lines like 112.

6. **Do not talk to strangers**
   If someone offers you candy, asks you for help, or wants to "talk privately"—say NO and walk away.

7. **Do not accept rides from anyone—not even known people—without permission**
   Always inform your parents first.

8. **Hold your belongings tight**
   Backpacks, water bottles, and gadgets should be zipped and secure.

9. **Use zebra crossings and follow traffic rules**
   Look left-right-left before crossing roads.

10. **Have a Safe Spot Plan**
    Know where to go nearby if you feel scared (police booth, shop, temple, school, etc.)

Try It

Street-Smart Scenario Game

What would you do in these situations? Choose the best answer.

1. You're walking home and notice someone following you.
   ❑ Run blindly
   ✔ Go into a nearby shop and call a trusted adult

2. A car stops near you and someone offers you a ride.
   ❑ Say yes if they look nice
   ✔ Say no, walk away quickly, and report it

3. You're lost in a market.
   ❑ Cry silently
   ✔ Go to a safe place (help desk/shop), ask for help, call home

"Find the Safe Spot" Challenge

With your parent or teacher, walk around your neighbourhood or school and:

- Spot 3 safe places you could run to
- Identify 2 public helpers (shopkeeper, security guard)
- Practice what to say if you need help:

"Hi, I feel unsafe. Can I please call my parents?"
Write down the safe spots in your Safety Journal.

The Buddy System

Always try to:

- Walk or cycle in pairs
- Go to the park with a friend or sibling
- Wait at bus stops or van stands with known people

Being in a group is always safer than being alone. Plus, you can help each other in emergencies.

"Two alert kids are better than one scared kid."

What Should You Say in Public Danger?

Use your voice wisely:

- "Help! I don't know this person!"
- "Leave me alone!"

• "This is not my parent/uncle!"
• "Stop touching me!"
Say it loud, say it strong. People around you will notice and come forward.

Think & Reflect

• Have you ever felt unsafe in a public place? What did you do?
• Do you always carry a charged phone or emergency contact?
• What would you do if you got separated from your group during a school trip?
• Can you name three places near your school where you can go for help?

Let's Revise

Quick recap of staying safe in public:
✔ Be aware and alert at all times
✔ Avoid lonely paths—choose busy, safe routes
✔ Use your voice to call for help
✔ Never accept gifts or rides from strangers
✔ Trust your instincts—move away if something feels wrong
✔ Know local safe spots and emergency numbers
✔ Walk with friends, not alone
✔ Keep your belongings close and zipped

Check Yourself

Multiple Choice Questions:

1. What should you do if a stranger tries to give you chocolate?
   • Take it politely
   • Run home without telling anyone
   • Say "No", walk away, tell a trusted adult ✔

2. Where should you NOT walk alone?
   - Crowded park
   - Empty lane at night ✔
   - Near your school

3. If you feel someone is following you, what should you do?
   - Keep walking slowly
   - Go to the nearest safe place and call home ✔
   - Ask the person why they are following you

True or False:

4. Being in a group is safer than being alone. **True**
5. You should always look at your phone while walking. **False**
6. You can trust anyone who smiles at you. **False**
7. Using your voice can help you stay safe. **True**

Creative Corner:

Design a "Street Safety Poster" with the title:
"Walk Smart, Stay Safe!"

Include tips like:

- Look both ways
- Don't take shortcuts
- Say NO to strangers
- Know your safe spots

Beyond the Book

Map Your Safety Zone
With your family:

- Draw a map of your walk to school, tuition, or park
- **Mark:**
    - o "Safe houses" (people you trust)
    - o "Danger zones" (quiet areas, broken streetlights)

o "Helpers" (watchman, vendors, shopkeepers)
Paste this in your room for daily review.

Practice Your "Walk Safe" Route

Once a month, practice your public safety routine:

- Look for escape paths
- Time yourself on how fast you can reach help
- Role-play what to say if stopped by a stranger

Bonus: Teach the same to a younger friend or sibling!

Real-Life Story: Ayaan's Quick Thinking

Ayaan, 9, was at a bookstore when he noticed someone staring at him. He quickly went to the cashier and said, "I feel uncomfortable. Can I call my mom?"
The staff helped him call his mother. Later, it was found the man had followed other kids too.
Because of Ayaan's awareness and courage, many children stayed safe.

Words to Learn (Glossary)

Word	**Meaning**
Public Safety	Staying safe in open, public places like streets and parks
Stranger	Someone you don't know well or trust
Alert	Watching and listening carefully
Emergency	A sudden problem where you need help quickly
Instinct	A feeling that something is not right, even if you can't explain it

Chapter 10

Bully-Proof Skills Every Kid Should Know

Ridhi was excited to join a new school. But by the end of the first week, she felt sad. A group of kids kept teasing her, calling her names, and once even took her lunchbox. Ridhi didn't want to go to school anymore.

Her parents noticed and asked her gently what happened. After she shared her story, they talked to her teachers. The school counsellor taught Ridhi how to stand up to bullies without fighting—by using her voice, body, friends, and confidence.

This chapter is for every child who has ever felt afraid, embarrassed, or lonely because of a bully. You are not alone, and yes—you can be bully-proof.

Explore

What Is Bullying?

Bullying is when someone repeatedly:

- Teases or calls you names
- Pushes or hurts you physically

• Spreads rumours about you
• Leaves you out on purpose
• Sends mean messages online
• Threatens you

"One-time teasing is rude. Repeating it to hurt someone is bullying."

Types of Bullying

Type	What It Looks Like
Verbal	Name-calling, mocking, teasing
Physical	Hitting, kicking, pushing
Social/Emotional	Ignoring, spreading gossip, excluding
Cyberbullying	Online insults, threats, sharing pictures without permission

Bullies try to make you feel small, scared, or powerless. But remember—you always have power to protect yourself and get help.

Why Do People Bully?

• They may be angry or insecure
• They want attention or control
• They think it's funny
• They've been bullied themselves
• They want to look powerful

But that's not your fault. Nobody deserves to be bullied—ever.

Bully-Proof Self-Defence Skills

Self-defence doesn't mean hitting back. It means using smart ways to stop bullying and stay strong. Let's learn how.

1. Use Your Voice

• Say "Stop it. I don't like that."
• Use a strong, steady tone
• Don't shout or cry—be firm and clear

2. Use Your Body Language

• Stand tall, head up
• Keep eye contact
• Don't look down or slouch
• Don't show fear—they're looking for it!

3. Walk Away

• Bullies want a reaction. Don't give it.
• Turn around confidently and leave
• Go to a group or an adult
• It's not running away—it's choosing your safety

4. Stick with a Buddy

• Bullies are less likely to trouble you in a group
• Stay with friends between classes, in the canteen, or on the playground

5. Plan a Comeback

You can prepare phrases to respond calmly:

• "That's not okay."
• "I don't think that's funny."
• "Leave me alone."
• "I'm walking away now."

Bonus Tip: Say it once, then leave. Don't keep arguing.

6. Talk to an Adult

• Tell a teacher, parent, school counsellor, or coach
• It's not tattling—it's reporting bad behaviour
• If the first adult doesn't help, tell another. And another.

Try It

Role Play: Beat the Bully with Confidence

Practice with a friend or sibling:

1. A classmate calls you a rude name in front of others
2. A group pushes you in the lunch line
3. Someone spreads a false story about you
4. A bully posts a photo of you online

Try different responses:

- Calm voice
- Firm posture
- Walking away
- Reporting the situation

Reflect: Which response made you feel strong?

"I Am Brave" List

Write down 5 reasons why you are confident, loved, and strong. Keep the list in your diary or bag.

Example:

1. I'm a great friend
2. I know how to stay calm
3. I speak up when something feels wrong
4. I'm kind and don't give up
5. I'm learning how to protect myself

What If You See Someone Else Being Bullied?

Be an upstander, not a bystander

- Stand beside them and say, "Hey, let's go."
- Tell a teacher
- Sit with them during lunch

• Send a kind message later
• Remind them they are not alone
Helping one person can change everything for them.

Think & Reflect

• Have you ever been bullied or seen someone being bullied?
• What would you do differently now?
• Why is it better to walk away than shout back?
• Who are the adults in your life you can talk to if something feels wrong?

Let's Revise

✔ Bully-Proof Checklist:
✔ Use your voice to say "Stop!"
✔ Show confidence in posture and tone
✔ Walk away from trouble, don't engage
✔ Stick with buddies whenever possible
✔ Tell an adult you trust
✔ Don't keep silent—talk, share, get help
✔ Never blame yourself—you deserve respect

Check Yourself

Multiple Choice Questions:

1. What is bullying?
    • A one-time joke
    • Repeated hurtful behaviour meant to harm ✔
    • Just playing around

2. What's the best first response to a bully?
    • Hit back
    • Use your voice, then walk away ✔
    • Ignore and cry

3. If someone is bullied in your class, you should:
    - Laugh to fit in
    - Be kind, support, and report ✔
    - Pretend you didn't see it

True or False:
4. Bullying only happens offline **False**
5. It's weak to report bullying. **False**
6. Strong posture can stop bullying. **True**
7. You can be confident even without fighting. **True**

Creative Corner:

Draw a comic strip showing a child:
- Being bullied
- Standing up with confidence
- Getting help
- Ending the bullying

Title: "I Am Bully-Proof!"

Beyond the Book

Bully-Proof Pledge

Say this aloud with your class or at home:
"I promise to stand tall, speak up, and help others.
I will not bully or support bullying.
I will protect myself and those around me.
I am brave, kind, and strong."
Sign and stick it on your notebook cover.
Family Talk Time

Ask your parents:
- Were you ever bullied as a child? What did you do?

• What should I do if I feel bullied and afraid?
Make a list of three trusted adults you can talk to in any situation.

Real-Life Story: Parth Finds His Voice

Parth, age 10, was new to his school. Some boys kept teasing him and pulling his bag. At first, he stayed silent. One day, Parth stood up, looked them in the eye, and said, "Stop. I don't like this." Then he walked straight to his teacher and explained everything.
The teacher spoke to the boys and their parents. The bullying stopped. Parth became a role model for standing up without fighting.

Sometimes, courage is just one sentence spoken with strength.

Words to Learn (Glossary)

Word	**Meaning**
Bullying	Repeated behaviour meant to hurt someone
Upstander	A person who helps stop bullying and supports others
Cyberbullying	Bullying using phones, games, or internet
Comeback	A smart, calm response to rude comments
Confidence	A strong belief in yourself and your abilities

Summary

Let's Stay Safe and Strong!

Self-defence is not just about punching or kicking—it's about using your mind, voice, and body smartly. It's about being confident, alert, and ready to act if something feels wrong. Through all the chapters in this book, you have learned that real power comes from awareness, confidence, smart thinking, and preparation.
Let's quickly revise the big ideas from each chapter!

Chapter Highlights

Chapter 1: What Is Self-Defence?

- Self-defence means protecting yourself from harm.
- It is not about fighting back—but staying safe.
- You can use your body, voice, mind, and actions.
- Everyone—boys, girls, big or small—can learn it.

Chapter 2: Knowing Your Safe Circle

- Some people are part of your "Safe Circle"—trusted adults like parents, teachers, or guardians.
- Learn the difference between good touch and bad touch.
- Know how to say "No!" and tell someone if something feels wrong.

Chapter 3: Awareness is Your First Shield

- Always look, listen, and stay alert to your surroundings.
- Use your five senses and trust your "gut feeling."
- Scan every new place you go. Awareness = early safety.

Chapter 4: Using Your Voice – Loud and Clear!

- Your voice is your superpower.
- Say "STOP!" loudly and clearly if someone is bothering you.
- Use confident words and posture to protect yourself.

• Practice being assertive, not aggressive.

Chapter 5: The Power of Posture and Body Language

• Stand tall, make eye contact, and walk with confidence.
• Bullies are less likely to target kids who look strong.
• Your body language sends a message—make it bold and brave.

Chapter 6: Safe Moves and Escape Tricks

• Learn simple escape moves like twisting out of a grab.
• Practice stomp, push, and run techniques.
• Use everyday objects like a backpack to defend yourself.

Chapter 7: Stranger Danger and How to Deal With It

• Never go anywhere with someone you don't know—even if they seem friendly.
• Use the "NO, GO, YELL, TELL" rule if approached.
• Create a safety plan for going to and from school or classes.

Chapter 8: Online Safety is Real Safety

• Don't share personal info online—like photos, school name, or address.
• Tell an adult if someone online makes you uncomfortable.
• Be kind online—cyberbullying is real and harmful.

Chapter 9: Confidence is the Key

• Self-defence starts in your mind.
• Believe in yourself and your ability to stay safe.
• Practice positive self-talk and celebrate your strengths.

Chapter 10: Bully-Proof Skills Every Kid Should Know

• Use calm, strong words like "Stop it. That's not okay."
• Walk away from bullies and tell a trusted adult.
• Stand up for yourself and your friends.
• You are not alone—help is always available.

Final Thoughts

Dear young protector,
You are brave, smart, and capable. Whether it's a push in the corridor or a message online, you now have the tools to stand tall, speak up, and protect yourself and others. This book isn't just about safety—it's about building courage, respect, and kindness.

Remember:
"You don't have to be big to be brave. You just have to believe in yourself."
So, stand tall.
Speak up.
And always—stay safe, stay strong!

Glossary

Here's a list of important words and their meanings from the book:

Word	Meaning
Self-Defence	Protecting yourself from harm using your voice, body, and mind.
Safe Circle	Trusted adults you can turn to when you need help.
Good Touch	A touch that makes you feel safe and loved (like a hug from a parent).
Bad Touch	A touch that feels uncomfortable, wrong, or scary.
Awareness	Being alert and paying attention to people and surroundings.
Instinct/Gut Feeling	A strong feeling that tells you something is not right.
Assertive	Speaking up firmly and clearly without being rude or scared.
Posture	The way you stand, walk, and hold your body.
Stranger	Someone you don't know or trust.
Cyberbullying	Bullying that happens using mobile phones, games, or the internet.
Bully	Someone who tries to hurt or scare others again and again.
Upstander	A person who supports someone being bullied instead of ignoring it.
Escape Technique	A move used to get out of danger safely.

Confidence	Believing in yourself and your ability to handle things.
Report	To tell a trusted adult about something unsafe.
Safe Space	A place where you feel protected, comfortable, and calm.